Contents

NO MORE

How to Tackle Procrastination with Power & Proficiency

By C.K. Murray

Similar works by C.K. Murray:

Confidence Explained: A Quick Guide to the Powerful Effects of the Confident and Open Mind

Emotional Intelligence Explained: How to Master Emotional Intelligence and Unlock Your True Ability

Master Mind: Unleashing the Infinite Power of the Latent Brain

ADHD Explained: Natural, Effective, Drug-Free Treatment For Your Child

Neuro-Linguistic Programming Explained: Your Definitive Guide to NLP Mastery

MIND SHIFT - The Key to Erasing Negative Thoughts and Unlocking Positive Perception

"You cannot escape the responsibility of tomorrow by evading it today."

-Abraham Lincoln

When it comes to life, we all have excuses.

We don't have the time, we don't have the resources, we don't have the motivation. Stressors are ignored, issues are forgotten, and in the long-term, as we convince ourselves of our 'reasons' for procrastinating, our minds are filled with one feeling and one feeling only: regret.

The truth is, everybody procrastinates. Whether something as small as avoiding a phone call, or something as big as delaying an all-too-important doctor visit, we all know what it's like to *dis*like our duties and our have-tos. For some of us, responsibility comes and goes, not always where it should be and not always where we want it. For others, life comes tumbling hopelessly apart, a direct result of our inability to do *what* we have to do, *when* we have to do it.

Some of us simply don't *want* to do what we have to do.

"I'm too tired," we tell ourselves and others. "I'll do it later."

"I'm too busy," we often say, rationalizing our lack of planning. "I'll get around to it," we might think, even if our true intentions are far from this reality.

In the end, procrastination can be devastating.

Not only does it prevent us from being the best version of ourselves, but it can lull even the most motivated of people, into the deepest of holes. As long as we don't have to think or do something *now*, we tell ourselves, everything will be fine. As long as we can worry about it later, then the present moment is preserved.

But this is nowhere near the truth.

Procrastination, at its smallest levels and its grandest scales, is *weakness*. When we delay on an important decision, our health, our well-being, and even our livelihood can be put at stake. We can miss a new job opportunity, miss a chance for a new relationship, miss a chance for happiness, for joy, for security and prosperity. We can miss the moment and forsake the future. In our worst moments of procrastination, we may very well miss out on a once-in-a-lifetime opportunity.

Could you live with yourself?

Truth be told, procrastinators are everywhere. Weak minds are a dime a dozen, and all you have to do is open your eyes and you'll see. Procrastination runs from the bottom to the very top. Procrastination affects nations. It affects economics, policy-making; the social shifts, the cultural trends—everything that defines and positions people for better living.

Procrastination affects personal finances. It puts us in debt, it keeps us from buying our dream home, reaching our dream vacation, and enjoying our dream retirement.

Procrastination costs us money, plain and simple. In fact, <u>H&R Block</u> estimates that the average tax procrastinator will miss out on $400 due to errors through rushing—a total of over $470 million in overpayments. When we procrastinate, whether world leader or average Joe, we create a pattern. And with each successive excuse, that pattern becomes fixed; a habit that is so engrained, so automatic, that it becomes part of our identity.

In the end, we fail to seize the moment. Worse yet, we fail to *create* moments that could have been.

Although procrastination may seem like our closest friend, in reality it's our biggest enemy. And if you continue to struggle with it, if you continue to tell yourself you'll change, only to put off and postpone time and time again—you're missing the point.

It's time to change your approach. STOP BEING WEAK.

Cut the Crap-- No More Excuses!

The reason you're reading this book is because you're tired of procrastinating. You don't like the fact that you claim one thing and do another; the fact that no matter what you do, you just can't seem to change your ways. Maybe it's had minor effects in your life, maybe it's caused major troubles. Whatever the effect, you know that you need to turn things around. Sure, *occasionally* procrastinating gives you that late burst of adrenaline you need… But more often than not, it just leaves you listless and unmotivated. After all is said and done, you feel worse off than if you had just gone ahead and gotten it done.

This is why getting into the right habit is critical. If there's anything for you to consider, it's Isaac Newton's first law of motion:

Objects in motion tend to stay in motion, and objects at rest tend to stay at rest.

Put simply, when you're in the habit of doing something, you're likely to continue doing that something. Action feels good, because your body and mind get used to productivity. You enjoy the act of completing tasks, of reaching the goals and outcomes that you expect. However, when you are used to *not* doing something, you learn to accept inaction. It's harder to get your body and mind going. You feel lazy, lethargic, incapable.

In other words, the hardest part of the whole thing is not actually doing something—it's getting it started!

The reason we procrastinate is simple. People crave novelty. We want to do things that are new and exciting; we are *compelled* to do things that are new and exciting. On a basic level, this desire for novelty is built into our DNA. Think about it. If we were not driven to transcend the mundane, where would we be? We'd be sitting around, literally doing nothing. We've never take risks, we'd never pursue new avenues, we'd never do anything to further our minds and our bodies. Instead of seeking stimulating tasks and goals, we'd do the same thing over and over.

Put simply, avoiding the mundane is actually the reason we survive. If we literally never did anything new, our bodies and minds would deteriorate. Without new stimuli, our muscles would atrophy. Our bones and tendons and ligaments would weaken. They'd become accustomed to rote, boring activities and lose their ability to adapt.

Meanwhile, our minds would follow a similar downward spiral. Our neurons would no longer make new connections, our IQs would drop, our intellectual capabilities would stagnate; the power of neuroplasticity would never be realized.

This is why we *think* that avoiding mundane tasks is the smart way to go.

But there's a catch.

Too many people procrastinate on tasks that are actually the tasks they should be doing. By putting off these tasks deemed too boring and mundane, people are actually hurting themselves in the long run. They are preventing themselves from getting to those new and stimulating activities *beyond* the mundane. Moreover, they are creating a cycle in which they constantly get behind on all sorts of things, from relationships to bills to performance goals and health and wellness outcomes. Thus, it's no wonder that 95% of procrastinators report negative feelings. They endure mounting stress, increased anxiety and depression, and a general feeling of inability. They feel guilt, shame, regret, anger and a variety of negative emotions. Overall, their quality of life plummets.

Of course, this is not to say that all those who procrastinate are procrastinators. Only 20% of people are chronic procrastinators, but *all* of us, whether chronic or acute, have encountered the ill effects of procrastinating.

If you're wondering how *you* fit in among the worst of the worst, it's time to find out…

What Kind of Procrastinator are YOU?

We're all different, but we're also all the same. We all think that we're better off not worrying about certain things now when we can do them later. The problem is, later never comes. So then what do we do?

Well, chances are we end up blaming forces outside ourselves. We say that if it weren't for this or *that*...we point to factors that have no real bearing on our lives and accuse them of making things difficult. We spare our egos and our feelings by denying any culpability. We make excuses and we make them loud and clear.

The problem with procrastinating is that it does nothing for us. We like to think that we're practicing "time management," but this is just a euphemism; a bold-faced line of bullshit we feed family, friends, and our good ol' selves.

So cut the crap.

If you aren't sure how deep your procrastination runs, it's time to evaluate. Take a step back, try your best to be objective, and see which of the following apply to YOU...

* You convince yourself that 'contemplating' doing something is as good, if not better, than actually doing that something.

*You drift, aimless, never really having direction. Your friends and family may seem to have their paths in order, but you don't. And when confronted with the error of your ways, you deny, ignore, and attack. You're right and they're wrong.

* You wait for the 'perfect' time to do something. You always have a reason why you can't do it now or soon, and whenever the 'perfect' time comes, you again change your mind: "Actually, *tomorrow* is the perfect time."

*You don't like to do things that are complex or require more than a small amount of time. For you, they're not worth the time and effort. You have "better things to do."

*You get anxious and nervous about what you have to do, tell yourself that you have to do it, but never do it.

*You constantly contemplate the many 'important' things you have to do, even though most of these things could be completed quickly and effectively. You blow the small things out of proportion and often avoid the big stuff altogether.

*You struggle with multitasking. You get so caught up in doing one thing or worrying about doing one thing, that doing two or more things seems almost impossible.

*You have a very poor conception of reality. You think that easy tasks can be done in a second and difficult ones will take "forever" to do. Your lack of planning and practical thinking is the main reason for this.

*You have a tendency to daydream and think about things that are impractical. Instead of doing stuff, you're dreaming about all the other *stuff* you wish you were doing.

*You call yourself a perfectionist. The reason you can't do things, you say, is because they have to be perfect. As a result, you never really accomplish anything. The things you do finish are poorly done and things you care about you never do.

*You react to duties and obligations with immediate negativity. You are discouraged before you even begin.

*Your goals are vague or nonexistent. You think that completing *something*, at *some* point, is good enough.

*You reward yourself for completing a task, no matter how small, by taking some free time. This time goes from being a short break, to a long break, to an undeserved vacation.

*You are generally impatient and impulsive. Sustained tasks are your worst enemy.

*You are rarely satisfied with a completed project; and are usually unsatisfied while working on that project.

*Your attitudes, behaviors, and feelings of helplessness only get worse with time.

The main thing to remember when it comes to procrastination is that you are delaying an activity in a way that causes distress. This is different from prioritizing. Putting off laundry because your boss just called you into work is one thing. However, putting off laundry, when you have no clothes to wear, because you can always just wear your stinky undies a little longer—now that's procrastination. And just downright nasty.

A lot of procrastinators like to convince themselves that they were juggling various high-priority tasks, when in reality, they are merely delaying the inevitable. Instead of doing these things, they may spend hours compiling a list of say, 15 things. In the end, they might do 3 of these things, and then 'reward' themselves by taking a break. Several days or weeks later, the other things are still looming, and so what does the procrastinator do?

Creates another list!

It's All in Your Head! Here's Why...

Let's cut to the chase.

You procrastinate and you want to stop. However, you obviously haven't done a very good job of it, which is why you're reading this book. One of the main reasons you've failed is because you don't know why. You're unable to come to grips with reality. You procrastinate because you've made a habit of procrastination. You've gotten comfy in putting it off, because you think you'll feel good when you don't have to do it. More than that, you'd rather feel *bad* doing it later, than doing it now.

But this is madness. Why is it madness? It's madness because you already know that you end up feeling like crap about yourself, yet you continue to do it.

Why?

Doing the same thing and expecting different results is called insanity. Nothing's going to change if you don't change it. If you sit around on your laurels thinking you're going to just magically change—you're being a fool.

Let's examine why:

Boredom

This is the main reason why people procrastinate. They don't want to do it because it's "boring." If you say this to yourself, wake up. A lot of life isn't going to be a waltz down main street. You're going to have to do some things that don't excite you. You might find cleaning your room, your clothes, making appointments, going to the grocery store, going to work—you might find a lot of this boring. If you continue to hate the boring-ness of everyday tasks and duties, throw in some creativity! Listen to music that you like, imagine funny scenarios in your head. Learn how to embrace the moment and savor the basic experience of doing things. Instead of thinking what you could be doing or would rather be doing, absorb the power of the moment. Mindfulness exercises can help with this.

Lack of skills

Ever heard an employer say you don't have the skill-set they're looking for? Well, then you're more than familiar with this one. When it comes to life in general, skill deficits can be devastating. If you don't think you have the requisite skills to talk to a mechanic about your car and avoid spending $1,000 on parts you've never heard of, you're probably going to put off visiting that mechanic. If you think or *know* you don't have the skills required for completing a project, an assignment, or some other workplace duty, you're probably going to procrastinate. You'll spend more time dreading, fretting and thinking about how bad it is than doing it.

Lack of the right skills can be scary. The good news is, it can be overcome. Skills can be taught, they can be learned, they can be practiced and passed on. Too many procrastinators will confuse skills with ability. They'll think that you either have it or you don't. They'll assume that it's too much work, that things will barely improve even if they try. For this reason, they'll rarely work hard enough to make the changes necessary. And when they do put in the work, it'll be too late.

Amotivational Syndrome

This is the fancy word physicians use to refer to problems with motivation. Smoke too much marijuana? They'll say you have amotivational syndrome. Struggle with psychiatric issues and need meds to get going? Maybe you have amotivational syndrome.

Again, procrastinators—chronic procrastinators—differ from most of us, because they suffer from this condition. Not only are they unmotivated, but they're unmotivated by a lot of things. And to make matters worse, they view lack of motivation as somehow unique to them. They think that because they're unmotivated to do x or y, they shouldn't bother doing it. In their minds, normal people are always motivated and therefore a lack of motivation means that the activity simply isn't worth doing.

Truth be told, there is a lot of stuff most people don't like doing. Taxes, for instance. Or maybe… taxes. And then there's… taxes.

People don't like going to the doctors. They don't like having to fill out checks for rent and cable and gas and electric. They don't like dealing with their bosses' demands, or forcing others into unfortunate circumstance at work because the company's policies have changed. Come to think of it, there's a lot of shit that people don't like doing. A lot of stuff that people aren't motivated to do.

The thing that procrastinators don't realize is this: sometimes motivation comes from getting started. You might not have the motivation as a baseline, but once you force yourself past that initial point of unwillingness, once you get the ball rolling—so to speak—your motivation builds.

Not everything is going to be intriguing or make your eyes grow wide or your pulse pump or your mouth move in a *whoooaaa* fashion. Sometimes, things are downright sucky, crappy, mundane and mind-numbing. The beauty of doing these things, however, is the feeling that comes after. Once you do them, you can breathe. You can enjoy the fact that you're responsible, that you're getting boring junk done so you can get on to the good stuff.

This is easier said than done. Just be real. If you're prancing through meadows expecting shit to smell like roses, wake up. If you don't like people telling you to do something, wake up. Come to reality and realize that you're going to have to put up with things you don't like. And if you don't like this reality, think of it this way: As long as you put in your hours, work hard, and pursue your passions while staying grounded, you may one day carve the niche you seek.

Most of us don't have trust funds, butlers or personal ass-wipers. We have to clock in and clock out, day after day. For those who are smart and realistic, this boring, saddening habit can become exciting. Better yet, this boring, saddening habit can eventually stop… Assuming you've put yourself in a position to succeed.

And assuming you've done the *stuff* you need to get there!

So stop putting off boring stuff because you're unmotivated! Chase your dreams, and shoot for the clouds. But always, *always*, keep at least one foot firmly planted on the ground, in the 'real-world.'

Sticking it to the Man

Some people hate 'The Man.' They hate the thought that anybody would tell them how to live their life; that anybody would have the authority or *audacity* to control them with such indifference. These same people are the ones that wait forever to do their taxes, or have piles of unattended bills scattered about their homes.

This type of resistance is a known cause of procrastination. These procrastinators rebel against structure. They show up to work late, take extra long lunch breaks, blow off appointments and commitments and generally ignore standards and expectations. They unconsciously struggle with power structure and dynamics. They react prematurely instead of thinking through the repercussions of their actions. And this is the irony.

Their rapid-fire reactions are typically decisions hinged on one move: delaying. In school, they delay handing in assignments because they dislike the teacher. In work, they delay completing the projects and getting in touch with coworkers or clients. In everyday interactions, they delay their responses and make themselves unavailable. Whatever their reason for delaying, these procrastinators decide to delay immediately.

"Screw you, I'll show you… by not showing you.. anything… for days..."

They struggle to see long-term effects and only choose to see how such authority figures affect them in the here and now.

Of course, these reactions are ultimately futile. More often than not, these people end up losing. They lose their jobs. Their relationships come undone. They get thrown in jail, their 'cause' lost or forgotten. They get beaten down, they get swallowed up, they get tossed to the wayside and left to fend for themselves.

And at the end of the day, they're nothing but *losers*.

Fear of Failure/Fear of Success

This is why people get depressed. This is why guys drink too much, or women get too much plastic surgery, or that kid in high school with all the brains flunked out and became a heroin addict. Fear of failure is akin to fear of success. Both types of fears factor in a lack of self-belief. We believe that we can't handle what happens once we apply ourselves.

Consider the movie *Good Will Hunting* starring Matt Damon. In this movie, Matt Damon play a super genius. He's the kind of super genius that can do anything he wants, in any field, any career, with relative ease. However, instead of applying his brilliance, instead of succeeding and becoming the type of person that can change the world through his intellect, the talented Will Hunting elects to be a janitor.

He chooses to mop floors and occasionally and anonymously complete MIT equations that only 2 or 3 people in the world can do. He spends his other time working in construction, getting drunk with his dumb buddies in seedy bars in Boston's southside.

In this case, the reason for Will's lack of success is not lack of motivation and certainly not lack of ability. In this case, Will Hunting is afraid of what might happen. As his court-appointed psychiatrist notes, "I look at you... I don't see an intelligent, confident man... I see a cocky, scared shitless kid."

Despite all of his ability, Will Hunting is scared. He's skated through life, taking the easy way out and for the most part hiding his brilliance. The reason for this is his underlying fear. He's afraid of what will happen if he truly applies himself. He's scared that he might actually struggle, or worse yet, that he might actually succeed. He's scared of the pressures, of the expectations, of the new-found beliefs that will be heaped upon his unready shoulders.

Will Hunting puts off the inevitable. He *procrastinates* because he's afraid of failure and success. Despite everything he is capable of, he's scared shitless. If he tries and fails, he's not as smart or as good as he thought he was. And if he succeeds, if he succeeds massively, how would he ever outdo that? Everything from that point would be a relative failure...

Think about it. Even if you're not a genius, even if the thought of basic Algebra makes you cringe, there's no excuses. Do you want to change your life, supercharge your existence? Do you want to improve your life but you're afraid to take the necessary steps? Are you afraid of what happens if you actually go after something with everything you got? Do the words and doubts of others creep into your head at every turn? Are your own doubts louder than theirs?

Are you afraid how hard it will be if you *do* fail? Do you think it would destroy you?

Then you're not alone...

Get Your Facts Straight and Learn the Science—the *Neuro*science of Procrastination

The reason you're not alone is simple.

All procrastinators, whether chronic delayers or occasional slackers, are ruled by their brains. The biochemical forces responsible for these behaviors and attitudes are complex and varied, but they are certainly real. They have been studied by numerous researchers, and the studies speak for themselves.

When it comes to procrastination, the main areas of the brain and the many neurological mechanisms are critical. If you can understand how these areas operate in your personal 'system,' you can begin to battle procrastination on the front-line.

And speaking of *front*-line, the part of the brain most responsible for procrastination is the front part. Known formally as the frontal lobe, this area of the brain is most troubling in people with severe procrastination problems.

The reason for this obvious. The frontal lobe is the gateway to higher thinking and higher-order behaviors. Basically, it is the reason that humans are so… damn… smart. The frontal lobe has a ton of applications. It can help us think about the future, in terms of repercussions and consequences. It can help us weigh the best course of action in any circumstance or scenario, and it can allow us to make simple and complex relations between people, places, and things. It also plays a large part in keeping our emotions, thoughts and behaviors in line with what is typically deemed 'socially acceptable.'

Of course, the main reason that the frontal lobe is so powerful in procrastination is its effect on executive functioning, or our ability to *execute* tasks. In case you've never heard of executive functioning, it's time to get informed. Executive functioning plays a large role in a number of disorders and conditions, everything from the natural treatment of ADHD to the removing of depression and suicidal ideation. But more than anything, executive functioning is the reason that procrastinators cannot carry out tasks and reach their goals. When we cannot execute properly, our planning for the future is impaired. We judge things impulsively, we waver in our attention span, we struggle with inhibition, and we generally find decision-making to be overwhelming, even for the smallest of tasks.

Procrastinators have very real impairments in their frontal lobe, and thus, in their executive functioning. These impairments manifest as:

- Disorganization – They couldn't formulate a proper planner/schedule/itinerary if their life depended on it.
- Diminished Self-Control – They feel like they can't plan or execute anything. It's as if nothing is under their control, as if all external factors are forcing them into positions of inactivity and inability.
- Lack of emotional control – They struggle with thinking

rationally and proactively. They get mad easily, want to give up easily, feel like there's no point in trying.

- Lack of planning ability – Again, they don't think about the future in realistic fashion. They either don't know how to set goals, or they don't understand the importance of goal-setting. The future seems impossibly uncertain

- Inability to use metacognition – Procrastinators struggle with thinking about thinking. They're not good at knowing how to use their cognitive strengths and overcome their cognitive weaknesses. They have extreme difficulty with knowing when and in what way to apply their intelligence

- Impulsiveness – Procrastinators will make minor or major changes in the spur of the moment. They may do something simply because they 'want' to, even though doing so could be very foolish. This can lead to drug and alcohol abuse, risky sexual behaviors, and a variety of self-defeating problems and issues

- Distractibility – One instant they want to change the world, the next moment they want to go outside, the next moment they're trying to check their phone or Facebook or contact a friend who they just thought of. Staying on task is a *tall* task.

- Inability to manage time – They don't know what to do with their time, so most of the time, they don't do anything… productive. Instead, they sit around acting as if they should or could be doing something, but in reality they rarely do it.

The thing about procrastinators is that they suffer from what experts call, "Self-Regulation Failure." Their brains are actually wired differently from others', due to continued habits of procrastination.

Inside the brain of the chronic procrastinator, the reward/punishment system is out of whack. Procrastinators react less to rewards or punishments that are not immediately applicable. If doing something will not have immediate repercussions, the procrastinator is averse to that task. This task aversion is the reason that many procrastinators absolutely hate doing things that theoretically can be delayed. If the procrastinator deems that a task will not affect them until months down the road, they are likely to delay that task, day by day, until the final day.

Procrastinators are also more prone to anxiety. They are even neurotic in many cases, creating and sustaining irrational beliefs about life's many issues—small or big. Many procrastinators will feel significant anxiety when approaching a given task and will subsequently delay, distract or avoid in order to reduce that anxiety.

Many procrastinators will even **self-handicap**. This is a concept in which the procrastinator creates additional pressure as an external reason for potential failure or under-performance. This allows the procrastinator to then blame outside forces and protect his or her frail self-esteem. If you've ever struggled to do something on time and have blamed some outside factor—then you might know what this one's about.

Say for instance a student puts off writing an important term paper till the night before. Then, suddenly, the student's laptop dies, because that student also procrastinated on getting a new battery. In the end, the student ends up using a friend's computer and writes a quick and sub-par paper. When the student receives a low grade, instead of feeling inadequate, the student explains nonchalantly, "I could have done better, but I had to write it last minute because my laptop died." In this case, the student avoids damaging his or her self-esteem by blaming outside forces. If this same student had actually put the time and effort into writing a good paper, and still received a poor grade, the effect on self-esteem would be devastating. Instead, the student never had the opportunity—due to procrastinating—and can now protect his or self-esteem by using the 'out' of the laptop failure. This is a chronic problem, especially among underachievers who are insecure about their abilities.

Self-handicapping is also similar to **learned helplessness**. Learned helplessness is often enabled by friends, family members and acquaintances. Even professors or bosses can exacerbate this by making special circumstances or offering excessive aid. When a procrastinator expresses learned helplessness, he or she is expressing a lack of personal agency. The procrastinator will act as if nothing can be done. He or she will make small problems seem like monumental struggles.

At work, this individual is incapable of making the kind of changes that inspire personal sovereignty. Such workers may rely totally on coworkers or bosses for guidance at every step, and may even expect others to do the work for them. This behavior also manifests in young children with over-involved parents.

When parents complete school projects for their children, they are teaching their kids to depend on others. Such students will depend on others for answers, input, reinforcement, and will often display inappropriate emotional responses when, heaven forbid, other people aren't doing their work for them. In many cases, these students are so used to having others take care of them, that when they enter the real-world, they are utterly incapable. They have never developed the necessary skill-sets and do not know where to begin in becoming self-sufficient. Prime examples of this are full-grown adults who still live with their parents, depend on their parents, and do not realize that such dependence is abnormal and dysfunctional.

Of course, this is not to say that all procrastinators live in their parents' basements eating Cheetos. Many procrastinators are simply underachievers. While some people relish (and excel at) putting things off to the last moment, most procrastinators do not. Unfortunately, this is all part of the fight or flight mentality.

The fight or flight response is a basic part of our DNA, evolution's handy-dandy way of preparing our cavemen ancestors for saber tooth tigers, and big boulders, and wooly mammoths, and giant, strong, beastly things that can eat them. Back in those days, our ancestors either challenged the beasts to the death, or ran like hell.

But for us, in our modern, relatively comfy age, fight or flight is about emotions. When it comes to these emotions, another part of the brain—the amygdala—plays a major role. This region is a prime factor in the registering of feelings like fear and anxiety, and is inextricably tied to our ability to make sound, sustainable decisions. Sadly, those decisions are not always sound, sustainable, or even *remotely* rational.

When the amygdala triggers the fight or flight response, it does this to protect us. It is a threat response that gears us up for battle, or for avoidance. It helps to assuage feelings such as panic, doubt, fear, and others.

Think of your life and the times in which you procrastinate. Chances are, you're feeling scared of some impending scenario. So what do you do? Well, you either tackle the task head-on, in order to get through it and get it over with. *Or*, you put off the problem and do something else that is harmless and comforting. Instead of taking on that work project, you surf Facebook. Instead of approaching your boss about that raise, you continue to stare at your computer. Instead of talking over your problems with your spouse, you go to the bar.

The reason this happens is because the amygdala triggers the release of adrenaline, which can just as easily cause us to pick up a car and heave it, as it can lead us to do nothing. The impulsiveness caused by our amygdala means that we are likely to pursue behaviors that are immediately rewarding. Why tackle some daunting task when you can play Candy Crush? Why approach some hot and intimidating girl or guy at the bar, when you can stand *thinking* of approaching that hot and intimidating girl or guy? The amydgala is about the neurotransmitter dopamine, which is an important chemical that makes us feel good. It's why drugs give us pleasure, why social medial 'likes' make us happy, why sex feels good, why alcohol and drugs feel good, and why just about anything we *want* to do, makes us want to do it. Short term gratification is the name of the game, and if procrastinating can make us feel good in the moment, either on its own or by delaying feeling bad, then we'll continue to do it—no matter the long-term consequences.

Which is why the only way to stop *it*, the only way to think beyond fleeting, short-term feelings, is to find something even better...

Shut Up & Walk the Walk

If you want to stop procrastinating, you need to stop talking.

Stop feeding yourself the same line of nonsense that's gotten you nowhere. Don't tell yourself "I'll do it later," because you won't. Don't tell yourself that you're "too tired," because you aren't.

Don't tell yourself anything.

The only words that should ring about your head are not statements, but questions. Ask yourself, simply: "How do I change?"

Don't know? Good, you're not alone.

So here' s how:

Small steps before leaps

Most people are too afraid to leap, and sometimes when they do they end up falling hard. Instead of trying to 'bust out' a task or project in a final act, break it into it component parts.

Remember, procrastinators are impulsive. They want instant gratification, and if you can break your task into small pieces, you can *trick* your mind into thinking it's getting instant gratification. Not to mention, you'll see just how easy the problem becomes when it's reduced to a series of steps.

Think about how you can break down your problem. Work project? Break it into stages, such as (1) planning (2) researching (3) synthesizing (4) part a (5) part b (6) part c—you get the picture.

The trick is to remember that working smart is better than working hard. Once you get rolling on the project, each component will be like a separate reward. You'll feel good about completing the first small part, and then start the next one, then the next one, and the next one, and so on.

Don't think about what's coming next until you're done the task you're on. This should be easy for procrastinators, since they're naturally bad at planning ahead anyway.

New Settings

Psychologists have identified something called *context dependent learning*. This means that we can recall and exhibit learning best when in the same environment that we learned it. There is also *state dependent learning*. What this means is that you recall and exhibit learning best when in the same state that you learned it.

What this means is simple. If you're not in a productive environment and mental state, change that state. Drink some coffee, reorganize your room, make sure that you're not in a place that is distracting. Create an environment where you are motivated to work. Don't go somewhere where you'll run into others. Don't go somewhere where you want to sleep or rest. Don't go somewhere where you're tempted to watch TV. or surf the internet.

Think about what you're trying to get done. If you drank coffee when you were studying for a test, drink coffee before you take the test. And if you can study in that room in after-class hours, do so. That way you'll be better able to recall details when taking the test in that room. Remember, state-dependent and context dependent learning.

If you are procrastinating on calling a client or talking to someone else, make sure to always call this individual from the same setting. It will become a comfortable habit and you won't feel awkward about doing it.

Think about the environment and state that optimizes your willingness to do something. If you want to clean out your workplace or home space, make sure to be in the same mental state that you were in when you've done it before. If this means eating chocolate donuts, eat chocolate donuts. If it means having your Ipod, listen to your music. If it means getting up early or doing it in the wee hours late at night, feel free to do so.

Think about what state gets you in the mood for exercising and working hard. Consider what motivates you to lose weight and stay fit. What motivates you to keep up on your relationships and correspondences? What makes you focused on your finances and budgeting? Consider what has worked in the past and what hasn't—and stick to the tried and true!

And if you've *never* had success sticking to a particular task, try something completely different. Research shows that the best time to get stuff done is the *exact* time we consider the worst for getting stuff done.

Know an Achiever

Befriend somebody who is motivated, somebody who sticks to their guns and doesn't make excuses. Somebody who is mentally and physically healthy, somebody who you look up to, but who you can talk to. Try to find somebody outside your family, somebody with whom you can discuss everyday and even personal issues. Find a confidante and a hard-worker. You want somebody who takes a genuine interest in your happiness and success. You want a person who also takes a genuine interest in his or her own success. You don't want somebody who is successful but selfish. The more self*less*, the better.

This is the trick. If you can find somebody like this—maybe a coworker, maybe a long-time friend—you will find yourself highly motivated. The two of you can hold each other accountable. More than that, you can bounce fresh ideas and perspectives off one another without feeling threatened or antagonized.

You also want to tell this person about your goals. This ensures that he or she is always asking about your progress, and keeping you honest. Know what you're doing and do it right—steady, strong-willed progress.

Write it Down

Don't write some vague bogus list that you'll never adhere to. Get serious and be specific. Write specific deadlines and end-dates. Make it progressive, so that each goal works toward a smaller goal. Follow these steps and make sure that they are *necessitated*. In other words, make sure that failure to achieve one goal—no matter how small—will ruin your entire overall goal. This creates a sense of necessity so that you'll actually do it on time. Feel free to have daily, weekly, monthly, yearly and even lifetime goals.

Make sure that they are interconnected.

Delete Distractions

We oftentimes set ourselves up for failure, sometimes unknowingly. Don't allow yourself excuses. Deactivate your Facebook if you have to. Keep your car regularly maintained and filled with gas. Have your phone charged and your voice-mail open to new messages. Keep favorite websites less accessible. Close out tabs and hide distracting files and folders. Stay away from people who don't have your best interests at heart.

Keep booze and drugs at bay, or at least hard to access. Make sure kids and family are not there to pull you away from important tasks you *have* to do. Turn off your phone if you have to focus on something that doesn't require outside contact. Turn *on* your phone if you need to be readily available. Think about the ways in which you procrastinate and how these ways can be reduced or made more difficult.

Become Less Perfect

This may seem counter-intuitive, but really it's what you want. The reason procrastinators suffer is because they're often perfectionists. They wait and wait for the perfect opportunity that never arrives. They spend hours, days, months and years looking for that next great opportunity—only to never recognize or seize it when it comes.

But usually, it doesn't come. Instead, create your perfect opportunity. As the Nike slogan goes, "Just Do it." You'll feel better that you did and love yourself for doing so. Better yet, you'll realize that *you* can determine your success or lack thereof.

Still, be honest. Not all of us are going to be movie stars or famous writers or millionaire entrepreneurs or models or athletes—but we sure as hell won't know if we don't try. Don't fear failure. If you fail, you're no different than anybody else. Besides, it's only through failure that we recognize true success. Sometimes you have to mess up and fall down, time and time again, before you can find what truly makes you happy.

Life is not about reaching a certain point faster than others. It's about enjoying the ride. Because you never really know, when that ride might end.

Want to be Successful? Then Learn from the Best! – The Top Mantras of PROVEN Winners

Even so, enjoying the ride of Life doesn't mean settling for mediocrity. If you dream big and want something that others have written off as 'fantasy' or 'unrealistic,' don't be afraid to venture where others have been too afraid to go. Enjoy the process and shoot for the stars, just be sure to keep yourself grounded. Chase your dreams with real-word fuel. Use your money, your relationships, your strengths, your weaknesses, and your visions of future to move you forward.

And learn to lead.

Leading isn't just about controlling others or showing others how to get it done. Leading is about controlling your own destiny. Following your *own* lead.

See, leaders don't make excuses. They don't crumble when times get tough, and they don't go running to others when it's their own fault. Leaders are leaders because they know what it takes. They're accountable, they're powerful—and best of all, they're honest.

If they fail, they admit it. They own up to their bullshit and they work to fix it. Leaders don't sit around, dawdling and twiddling their thumbs. They don't expect others to change things, because frankly… other people are worried about other people.

Leaders understand the most important aspect of success: the self.

If your self is weak and needy, you will never be successful. If you can't take a hit and keep going, you'll never be successful. If you can't learn from your mistakes and see obstacles for opportunities, you're *never* going to make it.

Instead you'll end up like everybody else. Quietly and painfully desperate.

So don't be like everybody else. Wise up and work hard.

If you want to make it like the bigshots, if you want power, charisma, and the ability to tackle life's biggest problems with fearless ferocity, learn from the best.

It's called <u>neurolingustic programming</u>. You program your brain, your neurons, to work the way you want them to. And the way you do this is simple: find your template.

Templates are everywhere. They're the people we want to be like. Maybe they're star athletes. Maybe they're powerful men or women whose every word are drenched in confidence and certainty. Hell, maybe they're even family members or friends, people who we have witnessed personally; examples for future generations to come.

Whoever your template, learn to model. Don't mimic—you're your own person. Instead, *model.* This means taking your own life experiences, dreams, goals, etc., and acting how others would act.

If your template is your hard-working, smart-thinking father, consider how he made it. How would he act in the face of stress and duress? Would he crumble and give up? Would he doubt himself? Or would he go ahead with a realistic and unrelenting attitude, hellbent on succeeding despite his darkest demons and detractors?

If you don't know what it takes to be successful, now you know:

Don't wait for success, seize it!

Don't sit around. You have to start at some point, and the starting point doesn't even have to truly be the start. Some writers start their stories in the middle. Some business gurus work backwards. Some architects envision from the top down, not the bottom up. Where ever you start, what matters is the fact that you do, not *where* you do.

Don't work hard, work smart!

Burning yourself out is only going to hurt you in the long run. Learn how to work in bursts if you'd like, or learn how to sustain at a lower pace. Whatever your preferred method, remember that recovery is as important as working. The same thing that applies to physical exercise applies to mental exercises. You can't make gains if you don't allow yourself downtime to reap the rewards of your efforts. Success stories rarely happen overnight, and they shouldn't. Sustainable success is built on a foundation of intelligent work, forward planning, and unflinching belief.

Others are here to help

You're not going to get anywhere in life all on your lonesome. You need others, and having the foresight to enlist others' help is what matters. If you can put your ego aside and ask for the expertise of those in the know, you're going to improve. You won't improve right away, but you'll certainly be getting yourself out there. You'll learn people you can trust and those who could care less. You'll understand why certain individuals are successful and others are not. Most importantly of all, you'll know what it takes to get things going in the right direction.

That's what matters.

If you don't have time, you don't have a clue

A lot of people think that having things to do all the time means that they're getting shit done. This is not true. Being busy does not mean you're necessarily being productive. Americans have long work hours and short vacation times, but they aren't the most productive. People who seize success are the same people who take advantage of the right moments and let loose when it's time to relax. They know that wasting time on social media isn't going to cut it when they could be closing deals. They know that talking to a client about details that have already been covered is not going to further the business. They're content to disconnect from work when 'work' becomes wasteful.

Vary Your Focus

Learn to multitask smart. Understand that working on one thing to exhaustion is only going to wear you out and kill your creativity and drive. Move across different tasks, but try to give each task equal consideration. If you're constantly jumping from one thing to the next, you're never going to make any headway. Instead, focus on several high-priority tasks and only move on to other projects when you've completed your primary goals. Don't fret downsizing. Give yourself a rest, but be consistent about your main focuses. Along the way you'll probably find that your ideas for one project will come about when working on another.

The human brain is a wondrous thing!

Abstinence

No, this is not some hippie mantra. It's a very real and helpful way to get things done. Too often we are plugged into our phones, computers, gadgets and social media. These devices can drain our intuitive and creative faculties. One way to recharge our batteries is by removing ourselves from the batteries altogether.

Go out into nature. Exercise, or simply walk about the woods, your yard, a nearby park, stream or field. Find a way to clear your head by allowing the natural world to balance with the artificial one. This is a good way to get your head on straight and start thinking with increased lucidity. Besides, all the endorphins from exercise will pump you full of potentially genius ideas! Not to mention, putting your life into perspective.

Nothing says *worry less* than realizing we're all just cosmic dust on a rock floating in infinity!

So there ya go.

If none of this has helped you, you simply can't be helped. You're screwed and there's nothing that's going to change your ways. You might as well find the nearest bridge, calculate the proper physics, and ensure the fall ends it all…

But jokes aside, your life is going to change. No more will you feed yourself bullshit or look at things with excessive fear. You need to understand that your problems are created by you, to a large extent. If you aren't happy, if you procrastinate and can't seem to stop—you're wrong.

The reason you don't stop procrastinating is because you've created a habit. You've deceived yourself into thinking that it's better to wait, even when the vast majority of evidence shows otherwise. And even if you've occasionally had success in procrastinating, that does not negate all the times you didn't.

Procrastination is a dream-killer and excuse-filler. It's the reason so many people get behind on so many things. The funny thing is, if most of these people just took the time to change one habit, one day at a time, they would realize what they're doing. Too many times people look back and wonder how it went wrong.

What they don't realize is that their every decision, however seemingly insignificant, has led to their troubles. Losers aren't made overnight, they're made second over second, thought to thought, action by action. They're created by making excuses, by embracing bullshit, by imagining themselves as somehow outside the realm of human responsibility.

They allow their emotions to color their attitudes and behaviors. They allow emotionality to rule rationality. At the end of the day, procrastinators won't stop unless they start. Because if they don't start today, they never will. They'll let life slip by, moments to dwindle and times to run dry.

And after all the lies, all the half-truths and empty promises, all the self-deluding, self-defeating, self-handicapping self-talk… they'll finally realize…

NO MORE

A Special Note:

Thank you for reading *"No More – How to Tackle Procrastination with Power & Proficiency."*

As always, thank you for reading. And may you continue to live healthily and happily.

Sincerely,

C.K. Murray

Other works by C.K. Murray:

1. *Mindfulness Explained: The Mindful Solution to Stress, Depression, and Chronic Unhappiness*

2. *Emotional Intelligence Explained: How to Master Emotional Intelligence and Unlock Your True Ability*

3. *The Confidence Cure: Your Definitive Guide to Overcoming Low Self-Esteem, Learning Self-Love and Living Happily*